ANCIENT
EPHESUS

üney
B O O K S

Drawing of the Celsus Library.

Contents

Ephesus 4
Plan A of ancient Ephesus 8
The Baths of Varius 8
The Basilica 9
The State Agora 10
Odeion 11
The Fountain of Laecanius Bassus 12
Plan B of ancient Ephesus 14
The Temple of Domitian 14
The Fountain of Pollio 18
Prytaneion (Municipal Hall) 19
The Memmius Monument 21
Victory Arch with Reliefs of Hercules 23
Plan C of ancient Ephesus 24
The Fountain of Trajan 26
The Street of the Curettes 27
The Baths of Scholastikia 29
The Temple of Hadrian 31
Plan D of ancient Ephesus 34
Public WC 35
The Terrace Houses 36
Plan E of ancient Ephesus 40
The Brothel 42
The Round Tower 42
The Celsus Library 45
The gate of Mazaeus and Mithridates at the agora 49
Agora 50
The Marble way 51
Ephesus Theatre 54
The Theatre Gymnasium 54
The Stadium 55
Plan F of ancient Ephesus 56
The Arcadian Street 57
The Church of the Virgin Mary (The Council Church) ... 58
The Harbour Baths 59
Plan G of ancient Ephesus 60
The Artemision 61
The Church of St. John 64
Isabey Mosque 69
Ephesus Museum 71
Cave of the Seven Sleepers 84
House of the Virgin Mary 85

Published and distributed by:

GÜNEY KARTPOSTAL ve TURİSTİK YAYINCILIK

Kışla Mah. 43. Sok. Yavuz Apt. No: 1/4 ANTALYA
Tel: 0.242 241 97 97 Fax: 0.242 242 22 77
BRANCH OFFICE: Anton Kallinger Cad. İsabey Pansiyonu Altı
No: 2 Selçuk/İZMİR Tel: 0.232 892 68 42

Text: **İlhan Akşit**
Translation: **Enternasyonal Tercüme Hizmetleri Ltd. Şti.**
Drawings: **Özcan Atalay**
Layout: **Emine Dalkılıç**
Photographs: **Şemsi Güner, Tahsin Aydoğmuş,
              Turhan Birgili, Muhsin Demirel**
Colour Seperation: **Çali Grafik**
Printed by: **Seçil Ofset**

1 st Edition, 1994.

Ephesus

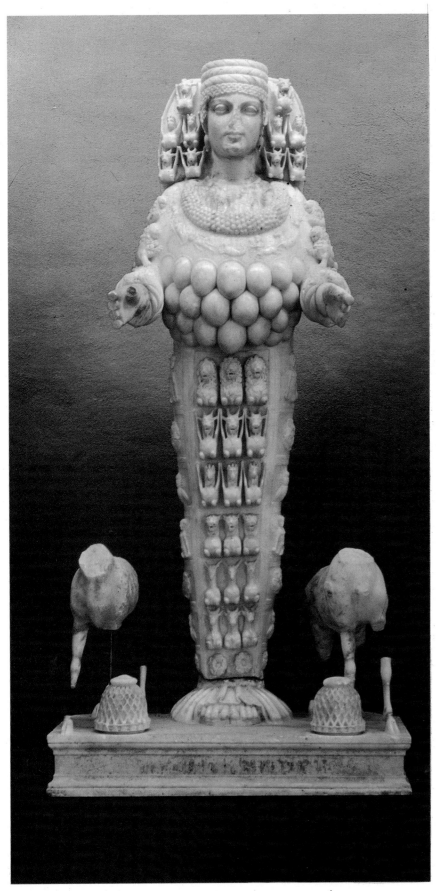

Ancient writers largely agree that Ephesus was founded sometime between 1500 and 1000 B.C., and this is supported by archaeological evidence at the site. Later, it appears that Ionians settled in the cities of Ionia. According to legend, under the leadership of Androklos, son of Kodros, the migrants arrived in Anatolia, and asked their sages where their new city should be established. The sages prophesied that a wild boar and a fish would lead them to the site of the new settlement. One day, Androklos, himself a new migrant from Greece, was cooking fish on an open fire, when a fish flew from the pan into the nearby bushes. Sparks from the fire also ignited the bushes, and as they flared up, a wild boar ran out of the bushes to escape from the flames. Androklos pursued and killed the boar. Then recalling the words of the wise men, he built his city on this site, which is at a place about 1200 metres west of the Artemision, where the original city of Ephesus was founded. The cities of Ionia were later joined together in a federation entitled the Ionian confederacy. Androklos, the city's first king, died in battle with the Carians, and the Ephesians erected a memorial to their first monarch. In the 7th century B.C., Ephesus was invaded by the Cimmerians, who razed the city to the ground, and burnt what they could, including the temple of Artemis. After this, Ephesus was ruled by a series of tyrants.

Throughout its later history, consequent to this early setback, Ephesus seemed protected from harm by the gods, and prospered either through chance or through the politics of its citizens. In the 6th century B.C., the Artemis temple was restored by the Lydian King, Croesus, who re-set-tled the inhabitants of around the temple. But when Croesus was defeated in battle with the Persians, Ephesus fell under Persian rule, along with the other cities of Ionia. One of the most important features of the city was

Statue of Artemis, 2nd century A.D.

that it was an important port which served to link Sardis to Susa. The Ephesians used this factor to their own advantage in many ways. Miletus, for example, had been destroyed and burnt down during the Ionian invasion, although it had been a trade rival of Ephesus. By deciding not to support the Milesians, they both strengthened their own position, and improved trade opportunities.

Alexander the Great showed a great interest in this city as he passed through Anatolia, largely because of the significance he accorded to the temple of Artemis. After Alexander, a similar interest was shown by his commander Lysimachos, who had the city's harbour, which had already begun to silt up at that time, dredged of river silt. Thanks to his efforts, the city was able to carry on as a trading centre for some time. Lysimachos also helped to build a new Ephesus as a fortified town between Mt. Pion and Mt. Koressos. These fortifications had walls 10 metres high and covered an area 9 kms. in length. The city was further expanded by migrants who moved there from Lebedos and Colophon. It was during this period that Ephesus was adorned with a theatre, a stadium and a gymnasium.

In 88 B.C., the Ephesians allied with Mithridates, the ruler of Pontus against the Romans, and succeeded in killing thousands of Roman troops, but later began to realise the extent of the Roman strength and changed sides. This made them not only an ally of Rome, but also caused Rome to appoint Ephesus as the capital of the Asian province. Until the 1st century A.D., the Ephesians enjoyed generally good relations with neighbouring states and with Rome, due to successful diplomacy. However, this did not protect them from the force of an earthquake which hit the city in 17 A.D., and destroyed it completely. During the reign of the emperor Tiberius, the city

Bronze Statuette of an Egyptian Priest 600 B.C.

Golden female figurine 7th century B.C.

was reconstructed and enlarged. Later, it was adorned with shrines and other buildings during the reign of Hadrian. The new city bore the definite seal of Roman architecture, in place of the Hellenistic city. It retained its political and mercantile supremacy during this period, and began to have religious significance during the Christian era, as it was said to have been the place of residence chosen by the mother of Christ after his crucifixion. However, the harbour began to silt up once again, and it gradually declined as a trading centre. Completely blocked with silt, the city became uninhabitable, and during the reign of the Emperor Justinian (527-564 A.D.) the inhabitants moved to the hills of Ayasoluk, where the same emperor built the basilica of St. John. The new settlement, which had been fortified, fell

View of the Celsus Library.
A view of Curettes Street.

to the Turks in 1090.

Now let us visit the Museum of Ephesus to look at the statue of Artemis Ephesia, the altar of the Temple of Domitian, the Socrates frescos and the Theodosian reliefs from the temple of Hadrian. After studying these beautiful artefacts, we may move on to the basilica of St. John on the slopes of Ayasoluk. This magnificent basilica was built during the 6th century A.D. by the emperor Justinian, and dedicated to St. John. The entrance to the basilica was on the western façade, and the plan of the church was cruciform. The narthex was covered with a single cupola, and the church proper with six domes supported on columns. Under the central dome was situated the tomb of St. John. On the eastern end of the church

Views of Ephesus Theatre and the Hadrian Temple.

were bays arranged in a semi-circle, used by the priests during ceremonies. The floors are mosaic, and to the north of the tomb are frescos on which are depicted several of the saints. In the centre is the figure of Christ, and to his left is that of St. John and a priest. The basilica has been restored several times, and on the capitals of several of the columns be seen the monograms of the Emperor Justinian and the empress Theodora. In 1869, an Englishman named Wood discovered the site of the Artemision. Excavations were carried out after this in 1904 by another Englishman named Hogarth. In 1895 the temple was first excavated by an Austrian team, and it is Austrians who are presently engaged in excavational work around the site.

ODEION (BOULEUTERION)

THE STATE AGORA

THE BASILICA

THE FOUNTAIN OF LAECANIUS BASSUS

Plan A of ancient Ephesus.
Ruins of Varius Baths.

The Baths of Varius

To the east of the Basilica is a large structure built of cut blocks of marble known as the Baths of Varius. Built with its north and east walls carved from natural outcroppings of rock, the baths were constructed in the 2nd century A.D. and restored on numerous occasions, of which the 40 metres long corridor covered with mosaics from the 5th century is in evidence. With its frigidarium, tepidarium and caldarium, and other adjacent sections, the baths covers a fairly large area. To the south of

THE BATHS OF VARIUS

View of Odeion and the Basilica.

the baths is a large public toilet from the Roman Period and other structures which were unearthed during excavations in 1969. This structure was possibly a gymnasium and Vedia Faedrina, daughter of Vedius Antonius, one of the wealthy citizens of Ephesus, and the famous sophist P. Flavius Daminianus each had a room added to the structure. The building uderwent major alterations during the Byzantine Period.

The Basilica

The Basilica, which starts from the Gymnasium before the Odeion and extends to the foundation chambers on

A view of Agora.

Its location next to the State Agora permitted commercial transactions to be carried out more rapidly. It has been established that to the east of the Basilica there was a stoa, which underwent major alterations. From here, there were three entrances to the Basilica of which the largest was in the middle. It was here that the statues of Augustus and his wife Livia, on display in the Ephesus Museum, were found. The Basilica is 165 metres long and contains columns with typical 1st century A.D. bulls' heads and Ionian capitals.

the west was originally devoted to commerce, having been constructed as an exchange. The Basilica was constructed in three sections during the reign of Augustus over a gallery with a single hall, which was located during the Hellenistic period. This is a typical Roman basilica, one unusual feature of which is columns, most of which were restored and installed here.

The State Agora

The square structure built immediately alongside the Basilica is the State Agora of Ephesus which is reached from the Basilica by four steps. This Agora, which was built during the Roman Period over the existing 2nd century B.C. Agora, was where all the city's business other than commerce was conducted. Exploratory excavations made in the northeast corner of the Agora have turned up a great number of graves from the 7th through 6th centuries B.C. and a stone-paved road, and a archaic sarcophagus of terra cotta was found here. From this it is understood that in the archaic period this section served as the necropolis of Ephesus.

The Agora is 160 metres long and 73 metres wide and appears to have been constructed during the reigns of Augustus and Claudius, that is, during the 1st century A.D. In the center of the Agora, a temple in a somewhat different style was unearthed in 1970. This structure, also from the 1st century A.D. appears to have been a Temple to Isis. Constructed on a 10 by 6 column plan, only the foundations of this temple have been located. The superstructure of the temple was torn down on the orders of the Emperor Theodosius in the 4th century in the course of alterations which were made in the Agora.

A different view of Agora.

Two different views of Odeion.

Odeion (Bouleuterion)

The Odeion, in which State affairs and concerts were held, was ordered to be construct by Publius Vedius Antoninus and his wife Flavia Papiana, two wealthy citizens of Ephesus, in the 2nd century A.D.

The Odeion seated an audience of 1450 and was enclosed. Since the podium next to the orchestra and the stage section do not conform to the style of a typical Roman theatre, the structure was most likely used primarily as a meeting hall for the Municipal Council. The location of government structures alongside strengthens this view.

The Fountain of Laecanius Bassus

On the southwest corner of the State Agora we find the remains of a fountain. According to an inscription which was turned up during the course of excavation, construction of this fountain was ordered by Gaius Laecanius Bassus in 80 A.D. The facade of this fountain constructed by Bassus, one of the wealthy man of Ephesus, was richly decorated, and consisted of two storeys which faced the street. The statues of Tritons and Muses, which were found at the fountain, are now on display at the Ephesus Museum. Because of the enormous size of the fountain it has been referred to as the "Water Palace". This fountain is connected to another fountain which is located just opposite it to the west of the State Agora, and also at the same time to a storage cistern. The main section consists of a body in the form of a semicirle and was built in the 2nd century A.D. The fountain underwent repairs in the reign of Constans and Constantius II (337-350) when the present wings were added. In inscriptions, this structure is referred to as the Nymphaion. It is the terminal point of the Aqueduct of Sextilius Pollio, which was built during the reign of Augustus between 7-15 A.D. The aqueduct was 3.5 kilometers long, and its remains may still be seen along the Selçuk-Aydın highway. There was a cistern in the upper part of the fountain, and the surroundings of the structure were decorated with statues of the Emperor.

General view of State Agora.
The Water Palace.

VICTORY ARCH WITH
RELIEFS OF HERCULES

THE MEMMIUS MONUMENT

The Temple of Domitian

The Temple of Domitian (A.D. 81-96) was the first structure at Ephesus dedicated to an emperor. The building is constructed on a terrace set on vaulted foundations. The temple was constructed by the Ephesians as a token and symbol of their friendship with Romans. Today little remains of the Temple of Domitian, which was located in the centre of a broad platform, exists. The work on the temple began while the emperor was still alive, and the structure was destroyed at the end of the Christian Period. The huge statue of Domitian found near the temple is today at the İzmir Museum. Approach to the temple was achieved by means of the monumental stairway still visible today on the north side of the

PRYTANEION (MUNICIPAL HALL)

THE FOUNTAIN OF POLLIO

THE TEMPLE OF DOMITIAN

Plan B of ancient Ephesus.
Entrance of the Domitian Temple.
View of the Domitian Temple.

terrace. The façade of the temple was decorated with eight columns. To the north was an altar, now on display in the Ephesus Museum, which is decorated with reliefs portraying various implements of war. The terrace is 50 by 100 metres in size, and from the north appears to be two storeys high. The terrace is set on a foundation which rests against the slope. On the east were shops and small chambers, where a fresco of Demeter was found. On either side of the U-shaped extension are niches, above which were located windows which served to light the interior.

Ruins of the Domitian Temple.

The Fountain of Pollio

This fountain was built in 93 A.D. by E.Atillius on behalf of E.Sextilius Pollio. The fountain had a large covered pool which was faced in marble slabs. This Odysseus and Polyphemus group of statues, recently uncovered at excavations still going on, display at the Museum.

The fountain has been restored from portions which have been found and raised.

General view of the Pollio Fountain, 1st century B.C.

The Pollio Fountain.

Prytaneion (Municipal Hall)

The Municipal Hall, built together with the Altar of Hestia alongside it, was at the same time used as the sacred precinct of the City.

There was a sacred flame kept constantly alight over the Altar of Hestia, and there were statues of Artemis of Ephesus here which were marble copies of the wooden statues located in the Temple of Artemis.

The Prytaneion was primarily a place where religious ceremonies and rituals were held.

Although the building was first constructed in the 3rd century B.C. during the reign of Lysimachos, the remains we see today are those of the sections which were reconstructed during the reign of Augustus. The four-cornered pit in which the sacred fire burned is a relic from the reign of Lysimachos.

The building is constructed in the Doric style and is surrounded by a large number of late-period structures which were used for municipal services. A great number of structural elements were removed from this building during the construction of the Scholastikia Baths.

Three different views of Prytaneion.

Memmius Monument.

Two different views of the Memmius Monument.
Reconstruction of the Memmius Monument.

The Memmius Monument

It is situated on a square beyond the Herakles gate, and was built during the 1st century A.D., during the reign of Augustus, by the Memmius family. Partical restoration has been carried out with surviving fragments. According to an inscription. The monument was erected by Memmius, one of the descendants of the dictator Sulla. During the 4th century A.D. a large fountain was built onto the north-west façade.

Victory Arch with Reliefs of Hercules

This victory arch with reliefs of Hercules is located at the junction of the Street of the Curettes with secondary streets. The monument was constructed towards the end of the 4th century, but no other parts of it have been found. If the structure to be completed, it would appear to resemble the Arch of Constantine in Rome. The reliefs of Hercules were originally made in the 2nd century, and were brought here towards the end of the 4th century from another structure.

View of the victory arch with reliefs of Hercules.
Two different views of the victory arch.

Views of Trajan Fountain.

The Fountain of Trajan

Next to the Hadrian temple, also on the
Street of the Curettes stands this
fountain, built in honour of the Emperor
Trajan (98-117 A.D.). The pool was 20
m. long and 10 m. wide. It has been
partially restored. Originally the pool was
flanked by columns and statuary. The
statues are now on display in the Ephesus
Museum. The façade overlooking the
pool contained a colossal statue of Trajan
in the centre, the feet of which remain in
situ. Parts of the torso were also found
during excavation. This is one of he finest
monuments in Ephesus.

Two different views of Curettes street.

The Street of the Curettes

This street, which starts at the Celsus Library and extends east to the Magnesia Gate, is known as the Street of the Curettes, and takes its name from the class of priests referred to as "curettes" in long lists found at the clerical school of chief priests. These priests guarded the sacred fire of the Goddess Hestia (Vesta). The street is decorated with fountains, monuments, statues, and galleries containing mosaics. On one side there are shops behind the columned porticoes.

The street assumed its final appearance in the 4th and 5th centuries.

The Baths of Scholastikia

The Baths of Scholastikia, which are located behind the Temple of Hadrian, were entered by means of a stairway alongside the temple. The statue seen in the large hall on the west belongs to a wealthy Scholastikia, who had the baths reconstructed in the 4th century A.D. The public toilets and brothel located alongside the structure were first constructed along with the baths in the 1st century A.D. It is believed that the baths consisted of three storeyed. An extensive hall which would have been the second storey has been uncovered along with another room to its north and a tiled roof.

The room in which the statue of Scholastikia was located used as a dressing room, and it extends to the stuccoed hot room (caldarium) on the north. On the left is the cold room (frigidarium). The marble floor of the caldarium is built over brick supports, and under it flowed hot water from the baths' furnaces on the left. The frigidarium contained a swimming pool, and was located alongside the dressing room. The baths could house a thousand customers, and contained a library and entertainment rooms. There is also a doorway opening onto the street leading to the Theatre on the east slope.

The Scholastikia Baths.

Three different interior views of Scholastikia Baths.

The Temple of Hadrian.

The Temple of Hadrian.

The Temple of Hadrian

This is on the street of the Curettes, and is one of the better preserved buildings at Ephesus. According to the inscription over the architrave it was constructed by P.Quintilius between 118-138 A.D., and dedicated to the emperor Hadrian. Corinthian columns on the façade support a triangular arched frieze, highly decorative in character, which contains a relief of Tyche, goddess of victory. A vaulted roof covers the colonnaded portico. Four statue bases front the building. Demolished in the 4th century A.D. during restoration, the two friezes

flanking the portal were brought from other buildings and mounted there. They represent scenes from the foundation of Ephesus, and include figures of deities and Amazons, and the Amazons and Dionysos in ceremonial procession. The fourth frieze portrays Athena, goddess of the moon, two male figures, one of which is Apollo, a female figure, Androkles, Herakles, the wife and son of Theodosius and the goddess Athena.

A view of the Hadrian Temple.

Detail of the Hadrian Temple.

The Temple of Hadrian.

THE TERRACE HOUSES

Plan D of ancient Ephesus.

Public WC

These were closets in the center of which stood a pool ornamented with large columns, and with mosaic paved all around. Stone toilet seats line the WC and a canal runs in front of the seats.

The Terrace Houses

Houses on the slopes behind Ephesus are to be seen opposite the Temple of Hadrian. Those on the upper slopes are reached via steps. They are situated on the slopes of Bülbül Mountain, with the roof of one house forming the terrace of that above it. They were inhabited by wealthy Ephesians, and are finely decorated with mosaics and frescos. Built in the period of Augustus, they were much altered and continued to be inhabited until the 7th century A.D., according to the evidence of excavations. Two of the insulae houses have been totally restored and are now open to the public.

Peristyle House I: This two-storeyed house covers an area of 900 m². It is a 12-roomed house entered via a flight of steps leading down to a hall (A1), to the right of which is another flight of stairs, flanked by a facet and basin, which leads to the other rooms of the house. A2 is reached via a passageway. It is the courtyard, with four doric columns in the corners and paved in marble. The remains of a fountain can be seen in the northern corner of the court. Beyond this are the halls A10-11, which have mosaic floors and frescos decorating the walls. The house dates from the 1st century A.D., but these two rooms were added in 400 A.D. One of these rooms is flanked by a staircase leading up to the upper floor of the house, and beyond that is another chamber decorated with frescos and with a mosaic floor (B7). East of the peristyle courtyard is a hall with walls 4 m. in height. Situated next to the entrance, this room is decorated with fresco scenes from the plays of Euripides-namely 'Orestes', to the left and the comedies of Menander to the right, namely 'Sikyonioi'. It is known as the theatre room because of these frescos. The other walls are decorated with figures, namely the combat of Acheloos, the river god, with Herakles to the left. The frescos in this room, which also has a mosaic floor, must date to the 2nd century A.D. The house also possesses a bathroom, to the south of the entrance hall (A.8), with the kitchen flanking it (A.12). Next to this are various small chambers opening onto the flanking street, and the service entrance. Artefacts found during the course of excavation are displayed in situ.

Peristyle House II: This is beyond the first house. It possesses two peristyles and is larger than the other houses on the insula. First built in the 1st century A.D., it underwent various restorations up to the 7th century. The main peristyle (B1), which possesses columns dating to the 5th century in the Corinthian order,

Mosaic of Triton from the Peristyle House II, 2nd century.

Mosaics of Dionysos and Ariadne from the Peristyle House II, 2nd century.

The Peristyle House II on the Slope.

flanks to the south, a long gallery covered from end to end in black and white geometric mosaics. Opposite this is a second gallery containing mosaics of Triton and Nereide. Triton bears in his left hand, the spear of his father Poseidon, while holding the reigns of the seahorse bearing Nereide in his right hand. These figures are placed before the vaulted open niche (B.6). The latter is paved with black and white marble in a basketwork pattern. Frescos on the walls include the heads of Dionysus and Ariadne framed by medallions, surrounded by trees, peacocks, ducks and cockerels. These mosaics are dated to the 5th century A.D., and are in extremely good condition. The vaults are framed to both sides by a fresco frieze depicting Eros figures bearing a garland. Other rooms of various sizes to the east of the

house are paved with black and white mosaic patterns and embellished with frescos of birds and floral patterns. The walls of two other rooms (B9 and 10) are decorated with fresco panels of muses, dating to the 4th century.

B11-12 is the dining hall. Niches set into the southern wall mark the wash-basins. They contain frescos which were restored in monochrome at a much later period. The kitchen is on the western corner of the house, and is decorated with frescos of fish and birds. The second peristyle (B14) flanks this hall.

The Peristyle House A on the Slope.

Fresco of a female holding a diadem at the theatre room.

The Peristyle House B on the Slope.
Plan of the Houses on the Slope.

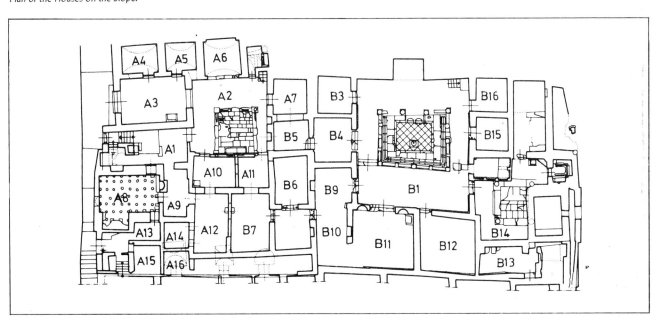

The Brothel

A peristyle house behind the Hadrian Temple is known as the brothel. It was built as part of a group of buildings, including the Baths of Scholastikia and lavatories, during the time of Trajan (98-117 A.D.). Its function was established with the discovery of an inscription in the lavatories. Entering from the Marble Road, a street sign in the form of a foot engraved on stone indicates its existance. A second entrance gives access from the Street of Curettes. The group of buildings of which it is a part underwent restoration in the 4th century A.D. It is a two-storeyed building, with a large hall on the ground floor, surmounted by a number of small rooms on the floor above, although these are now ruined. There are traces of frescos on the walls. The western hall was a dining room, and contains a mosaic depicting the four seasons. This flanks the two main chambers of the baths. The elliptical pool contains a mosaic in the centre depicting three women drinking, a servant standing, a mouse nibbling crumbs and a cat. The statue of priapos, with outsize phallus, now on display in the Ephesus Museum, was found in a well to one end of the building.

The Round Tower

This is situated behind the Trajan fountain, at the foot of Panayır Mountain. The tower was erected as a monument in 50 A.D. It is square-planned, and set on a podium was the cylindrical shaft surrounded by a row of arches on two courses, now in ruins.

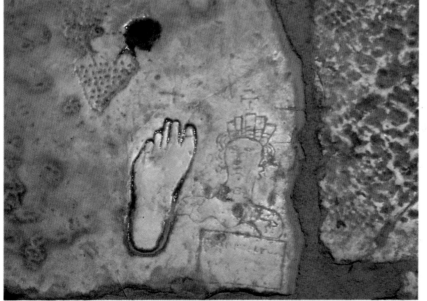

The Celsus Library seen from the Brothel

Footprint symbolizing the Brothel.

View of Celsus Library from the Scholastikia Baths.

43

View of the Celsus Library.

The Celsus Library

One of the finest structures in Ephesus, the Celsus Library has recently been restored. Raised on a high plinth, the building is approached via a broad flight of steps. It was built by the Consul Gaius Julius Aquila in 135 A.D. as a heroon in honour of his father, Celsus Polemaeanus, the governor of Asia Minor. The façade is highly ornamented on two levels, and there are three main portals. Over the portals were columns and statues arranged in niches. These statues were female figures representing the virtues wisdom, fate and intellegence. Niches on the interior of the building

Two different views of Celsus Library.

were designed to hold books. The tomb of Celsus was placed in a crypt below the central large niche. According to the inscription on the architrave of the building, its patron, C.Aquila, died before it was completed, and the construction was carried on by his heirs. Aquila left 25 thousand dinar for the acquisition of books for the library.

A view of the Celsus Library.

ΣΑΝΤΩΝΤΩΝΑΚΥΛΑ

ΕΜΑΙΑΝΟΝ   ΤΙΟΥΛΙΟΣΑΚΥΛΑΣΥΠΑΤ

ΥΠΑΤΟΝΑΝΘΥΠΑΤΟΝ

Details of the Celsus Library.

Statues of women at Celsus Library

48

The gate of Mazaeus and Mithridates at the agora

The most magnificent of the three entrances to the Agora was the gate alongside the Celsus Library which was dedicated to Augustus and his family by slaves, Mazaeus and Mithridates. The gate was constructed in 40 A.D. The dedicatory inscription in Latin belonging to the work is visible on one side, and was made in inlaid letters of bronze. The two prisoners originally were employed by Augustus and later by his son in law Agrippa. Subsequently they were manumitted and settled in Ephesus. After making their fortunes they had this gate constructed and dedicated in honour of their former master. Built in the form of a

The gate of Mazaeus and Mithridates.

General view of Mazaeus and Mithridates Gate.

ceremonial arch, the gate consists of three sections.

The second magnificent gate of the Agora was this one, located on the west. The front was richly decorated with Ionian columns, and the gate, which was somewhat high, was reached by a stairway. An inscription found near the gate reads "Whoever urinates here will be punished".

Agora

The broad area in front of the Theatre was the Commercial Agora of Ephesus. Completely surrounded by columns, this Agora contained three entrances, one from the Celsus Library, one from the front·of the Theatre, and one from the Harbour. In the form of a square 110 metres on a side, the north side of the Agora is left open, while the remaining three sides are surrounded by a portico which contained shops. The eastern and southern sides of the Agora were two-storeyed, the second storey of the eastern side being constructed in the form of an enclosed Doric stoa.

Originally built in the Hellenistic Period, the Agora was reconstructed in the 3rd century during the reign of Caracalla (211-217 A.D.). At the centre of the Agora was a sundial and a water-clock. The centre of the square was faced in marble and contained statues of the philosophers, statesmen, and of scholars.

Capital of column at Agora.
The Commercial Agora of Ephesus.
A view of the Marble Way.
View of the Marble Way and the theatre.

The marble way

The portion stretching from the Gymnasium of Vedius to the front of the Celsus Library has been referred to as the "Marble Way". Originally constructed in the 1st century A.D., this street was rebuilt in the 5th century with funds provided by a man named Eutropius. The western side of the street is enclosed by means of a well-decorated Agora wall. Since this street was set aside for vehicular traffic, a rather high platform was built for pedestrians over the wall on the Agora side. This covered platform, built in the Doric style, looked down on the Agora and on the street.

A view from Ephesus Theatre.

Views of the Ephesus Theatre and the Arcadian Street. 53

Ephesus Theatre

This theatre, which had a seating capacity of 25,000 was first constructed during the Hellenistic period, although the present structure dates from the 1-2nd centuries A.D. The Roman Theatre was begun during the reign of Claudius (34-41 A.D.), and it took 60 years to build. The second and third storeys of the skene (25x40 m) were constructed during the reigns of the emperors Nero (54-68 A.D.) and Septimus Severus (193-211 A.D.). Only parts of the skene now date from the Hellenistic period. The Theatre has three cavea, each 22 rows, to which access was obtained via flights of steps between the cavea.

The skene is 18 m. in height and the inner façade was ornamented with reliefs, columns, blind niches, windows and decorated with statues on three levels. The semicircular orchestra, surrounded by a channel, fronted a second skene supported on columns, 2.70 metres in height, which was approached by flights of steps. This section of the skene was used during the Roman period.

The Theatre Gymnasium

It was built in the early Roman Period and was named "The Theatre Gymnasium" as the building was used for the training of the actors of the theatre.

Festival at the Ephesus Theatre.

The Theatre Gymnasium.

Camel fights are held in the stadium during the festival.

The Stadium.

The Stadium

En route to the ruins after the Gymnasium of Vedius, the monumental gate of the Stadium attracts our attention. The original Stadium was constructed in the Hellenistic Period, and was restored and expanded during the reign of the Emperor Nero (54-58 A.D.). The large vaulted gates were later modified and repaired in the 3rd and 4th centuries.

The Stadium is 230 metres long and 40 metres wide, and its right side rests on bedrock. On the left, vaulted passageways have been constructed for the rows of seats.

Athletic contests, gladiatorial fights, and chariot races were held in this Stadium. The stepping stones of the interior have been carried away.

The Church of the Virgin Mary (The Council Church)

Situated next to the Harbour Corn Exchange, this is the first church to be dedicated to the Virgin Mary. It was also where the Third Ecumenical Council was held in 431 A.D., and so is considerably important to the development of Christian dogma.

The building in which it is housed, which is 260 m. in length and 30 m. in width, was used for scientific training, and for the theological training of the priests of Ephesus. The plan is that of a triple naved building, and in the 4th century the church was converted into a basilica with a central nave flanked by two aisles, when an apse was opened in the eastern wall, and a Baptisterium added to the north side of an atrium to the west of the church. The central nave is the same width as the apse, while the flanking aisles are somewhat smaller. They are separated from the nave by two rows of columns, with geometric-designed balustrade panels between. There are mosaics on the floor of the narthex, to the western tip of the building, decorated with geometrical patterns, while the Atrium, which has one absidal wall is paved with stones of various kinds. The Baptisterium is circular in plan, and contains the baptismal pool in the centre.

During the reign of the emperor Justinian (527-565), further alterations led to the construction of a centrally-planned chapel surmounted by a single dome, between the apse and the narthex of the original church. The cauldron in the centre was brought there from the Harbour Baths. In the 10th century a further church was added to the eastern front, with a small chapel being added to the southern tip of the church The council meeting held in this church in 431 agreed to accept as dogma the notion that Jesus, the son of the Virgin Mary was also the Son of God.

Apses of the Virgin Mary Church.

The Harbour Baths

Built in the 2nd century A.D., it was repaired during the reign of Constantine II(337-361). Oriented along an north-south axis, it stands between the harbour and the Gymnasium, and is one of the largest structures in Ephesus, measuring 160x170 m. and 28 m. in height. In the centre of the large hall to the east is the frigidarium, flanked on both sides by dressing rooms. The frigidarium contains a pool, 30 m. in length. Marble composite columns are set on piers 11 m. in height. Several statues were found there. The Caldarium, to the west, is a spacious, high-roofed building. Large numbers of statues were found in the baths, and their bases remain in situ.

The Harbour Baths.

mythology. The ruined Artemision contained a total of 127 columns, the 36 façade columns being decorated with reliefs. It was 115 metres long, 55 metres wide and 18 metres high.

The earliest traces of the Artemision building date to the 7th century B.C. The original temple was destroyed by the Cimmerians, and was re-built during the 6th century B.C. Destroyed once more during the reign of the mad king Herostratos in the year 356 B.C., Ephesus began to rebuild its cult centre on an even grander scale after that date. Alexander passed through Ephesus at about that time and learning that the temple had been destroyed and burnt down on his birthday, he expressed the desire to assist with its re-construction. He wished, the new temple to be dedicated to him. But the Ephesians

could not assent to this and undertook the reconstruction of the temple without his aid. The new temple of Artemis measured 105 metres by 55 metres, and was 25 metres in height, covering an area 6000 square metres in all. Alexander extended the temenos to include an inhabited area around the temple as part of the sacred compound. This sacred area was preserved through the rule of several different kings and governors, was expanded and finally abolished by the emperor Augustus. In 263 A.D., the temple was sacked and destroyed during the invasion of the Goths.

Column of Artemis Temple, Isabey Mosque and Selçuk Castle.

Columns of the Artemis Temple.

The Church of St. John

St. John lived here with the Virgin Mary after being cast out of Jerusalem in 37-42 A.D. according to legend, and it is thought to be here that St. John wrote his gospel, and was buried in the church bearing his name in accordance with his dying wishes. A wooden basilica was first constructed on the site, above his grave, in the 4th century A.D., which was replaced in the 5th century by the present church, built during the reign of the Byzantine emperor, Justinian (577-565 A.D.).

During the 7th and 8th centuries, Ephesus was under constant siege by the Arabs, when the church was surrounded

Main entrance of St. John Church.

Outer walls of St. John Church.

by a wall, which varied in structure over the years, but possessed 20 towers and three gates. The grand portal is the gate now used by visitors. The two other gates are to the east and west. The walls were built with stones taken from the Gymnasium of Ephesus, as if in revenge for the Christians thrown to the lions in that stadium during the first years of Christianity. The Church is entered via the main portal dating to the 6th century, which consists of an arched entrance

View of St. John Church.
Main entrance of St. John Church.

flanked by two towers, leading to a small atrium where one may see inscriptions related to the Church, which were uncovered there during excavations. This atrium, which measures 34x47 m. is on the western front, and consists of a central court surrounded by an arched portico with a balustraded gallery to the exterior. A number of amphora dating from various periods are to be seen in the centre of the court. A three celled cistern is buried below the western portal, and covered with a vault. This is buttressed with flanking walls to compensate for the curve of the site. Between the atrium and the nave of the church is a long narrow narthex. Massive lentils of dressed marble frame the three doors leading to the atrium and into the nave from the narthex. A wall and a number of portals were added between the atrium and the narthex at a later date, to create an exonarthex. Five cupola surmount the narthex itself. The main church is cruciform in plan, a classic plan with three naves, and a superstructure of six, large domes over tho main nave, with vaulted flanking naves. The domes were originally supported by marble and brickbond piers, still partially in situ, with a row of blue-veined marble columns

lining the Church between the naves. The monograms of Theodora, wife of Justinian, are engraved on these columns, which enables us to date the structure. The above mentioned rows of Columns are joined by a series of arches which in turn support a second row of arches at gallery level. The mausoleum chamber is situated before the apse in the central nave, and is marked out by being raised from the rest of the nave, with two steps between. A chapel, originally part of the treasury in the court, was converted for devotional use in the 10th century. The frescos of St. John, Christ and other sacred figures are contained in the apse. The treasury is reached via a gate immediately before it. This is a centrally-planned chamber, 6.30 m. in diameter, fronted by an absidal vaulted hall and flanked by a chapel. The main chamber is sub-divided by a cruciform plan, into a series of cells, each

Three different views of St. John Church.

containing vaulted niches. It is a two-course building surmounted originally by a dome, now in ruins. The baptistery is reached via a portal letting into the forehall of the treasury. It is connected to the Church via a long narrow corridor running parallel to the northern nave. The baptismal pool dates to the 6th century, and was originally a tomb.

The plan of the Baptistery is somewhat complex. The main chamber is octagonal in plan, and is framed by a narrow corridor and flanked on two sides by absidal-planned halls. The main baptistery is paved with marble, with the pool in the centre. The baptistery predates the Justinian church, being built in the 5th century.

The Church of St. John, the Burial Area.
Outer walls of St. John Church.
Main entrance of St. John.

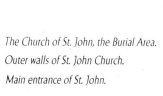

Portal of İsabey Mosque.

68

İsabey Mosque

This mosque, located on the slope containing Ayasoluk Castle and the Church of St. John, attracts the visitors to the latter structure with its beauty.

The Mosque was built by the architect Aliye son of Şamlı in 1375 on orders by İsa Bey, son of Mehmet, leader of the Aydınoğulları. The structure is built on a 51 by 57 metres nearly rectangular plan. The door which faces west is decorated with artificial stalactites, over which is a dedicatory inscription.

Upon entry there is a courtyard which is surrounded on three sides by porticoes with a fountain for ablutions in the centre. The Mosque itself is entered from the courtyard through a triple vaulted doorway. This section possesses two

General view of Isabey Mosque.
Portal of Isabey Mosque.

domes set upon four granite columns. The pulpit is covered with tiles. Three of the column capitals are done in traditional Turkish style, while a fourth is a Roman capital.

The western façade was done inspired by Konya Seljuk works. The upper parts of the windows on the left are decorated with rows of stalactites and inscriptions of hadith (incidents from the life of the Prophet). The ones on the right are each decorated in an entirely separate style.

This is one of the first examples of a mosque containing two congregation places, and as such it represents an important example of the transition from Seljuk to Ottoman art.

Drawing of a swashbuckler (Efe) of Ayasuluk

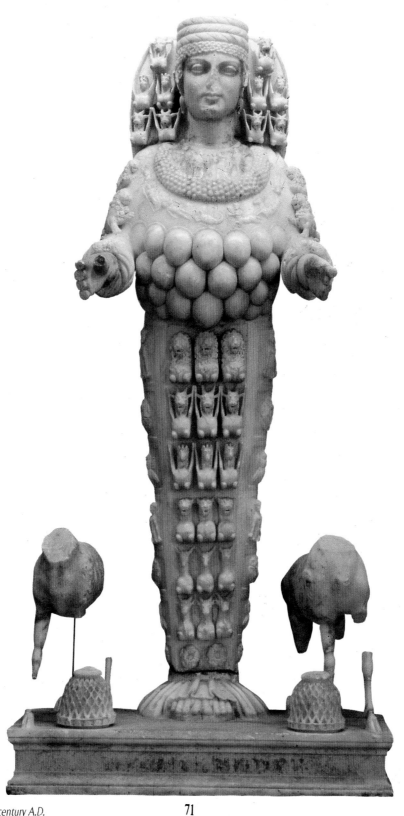

Statue of Artemis the Fair, 2nd century A.D.

Head of Commander.

View of House findings Hall.

Statue of Artemis.

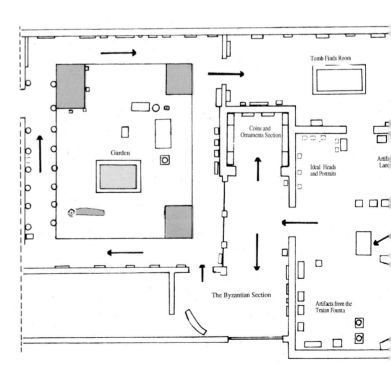

Plan of Ephesus Museum.

... of the Imperial Cults and portraits Hall.

A head of Athena, Marble, 2nd century.

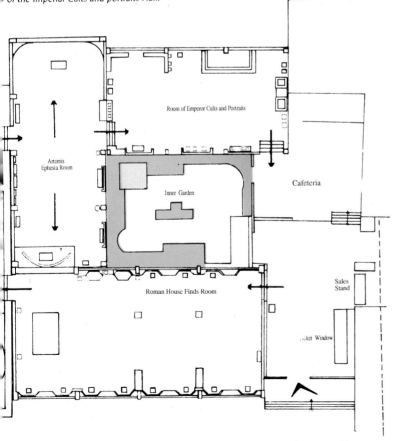

Fresco of Socrates, 2nd century.

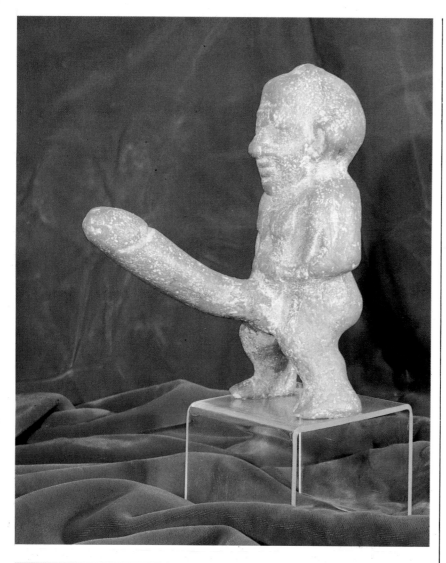

Ephesus Museum

The excavations which have been continueing since the last century at Ephesus, today are being carried out by Austrian archaeologists. The works unearthed during these excavations are being displayed at the Ephesus Museum. However the works obtained in excavations prior to World War II, were taken to the Vienna Museum. The works found during the excavations made after World War II were left at the Ephesus Museum. Therefore, a new building had to be constructed in 1964 for the museum which formerly was situated in a small building, the new building was further enlarged in 1979 to the present size of today's Ephesus Museum. The works brought from the ruins of Ephesus, the Temple of Artemis, the Ayasoluk Hill and the Belevi Mausoleum are being displayed in this museum. All of these are spread out in seven different halls.

The first hall is for household findings. Here, the frescoes found in the homes of Ephesus and the mosaics among which the head of Medusa and Dionysos of 5th century take place, draw attention. The most remarkable one is the fresco of Sokrates, the famous philosopher, made in 1st century A.D. Again the head of Sokrates made out of marble in 3rd century A.D. is also being exhibited in this hall. Another remarkable work in this hall which is on display in a showcase and made in form of the fountain of a pool is the small Statue of Eros with Dolphin which belongs to the 2nd century A.D. The waters are being poured out of the eyes of dolphin into the pool. Statues of Asklepios, the God of Health, of Artemis, small statue of the Egyptian monk of 6th century B.C. and the Statue of Bes, made out of baked soil in 2nd century A.D., symbolizing fertility are the favourite works of this hall. The most attractive one among the statues and

The Statue of Bes, 2nd century.

Statuette of Eros on a dolphin, bronze, 2nd century.

The head of Socrates, 1st century.

Bronze head of a man.

An Egyptian Priest, bronze 6th century B.C.

Head of Eros . A Roman copy dating to 330 B.C. of the Lysippos original.

heads of Eros, taking place in this hall, is the Roman Copy of Eros' head made by Lysippos in the Hellenistic period. Next to the child Eros' head, found in Bouleuterion, the portrait bust of Menander, the comedy writer takes place. Busts of Emperor Tiberius and the Empress Livia, Statue of Artemis and the bronze human head of Roman period are some of the other works of this hall.

From this hall, it is proceeded into a hall where findings of a small door and a fountain take place. The first work on the right hand side is the head of Zeus of 1st century B.C. Next to this, the statue of Aphrodisias of 1st century A.D. and in the centre the statue of a resting warrior of 1st century A.D. take place. On the left hand side of the same hall, the statue group of Polyphemos and Odysseus of 1st century A.D. can be seen. These works initially placed on the frontal of the Temple of Augustus, later were moved to the Fountain of Pollio. On the ground, the friends of Odysseus killed by the giant and on the side, Odysseus carrying a stake to take the giant's eye out are seen. Right across from this group, the statues of Trajan Fountain take place. Here statues of young Dionysus of 2nd century A.D., of Satyr in laying position (2nd century A.D.) and of Dionysus and imperial family by the wall are exhibited. On the other side of this hall, are the statues of Laecanius Bassus Fountain, also called the Water Palace. On the wall, the Roman copies of the head of a warrior with helmet and the head of Lysimachos of 5th century B.C. are some of the works which draw attention.

From here, it is proceeded to the hall of recent findings. Crosses, coins and the works of 1st century A.D. such as glass trays, theatrical masks, candles found in the Seven Sleepers' Cavern; the bust of Emperor Marcus Arelius found in homes

A table leg, featuring Dionysos, from Prytaneion.
The Bust of Tiberius.

on the slope are some of the works that can be seen here. The ivory frieze which is one of the finest works of the Museum was found in the homes of the slope in 1969. The work which belongs to 2nd century A.D. depicts the war, Emperor Trajan fought against barbarians. Emperor Trajan can be clearly identified in the high relief on the central panel.

From here, it is proceeded to the garden of Museum. In the frontal of a temple placed in this garden one can see the friezes of the Pollio Fountain completed and placed thereon. Also pillar heads, and on the west wall, tomb and vow steles are being exhibited here. The large sarcophagus which takes place in the

Statue of warrior resting, 1st century.

Statue of Aphrodite, 2nd century.

Statue of Aphrodite, 1st century.

Bust of Marcus Aurelius .

Detail of the ivory frieze, 1st century.

The Ivory Artemis figurine, 7th century B.C.

- Statue of Colossal Artemis, 1st century.

of 29.65x29.65 m. only its pedestal can be seen.

From the garden, it is proceeded to the tomb findings hall. Here, interment ceremonies and traditions, and also tomb findings are on display. Also, Mycenaean dishes found in one of the graves which dates back to almost 1400 B.C. and is located at St. Jean, can be seen here. In the middle of this hall, a clazomenae type sarcophagus of 5th century B.C., found in the Trade Agora of Ephesus and made of baked soil and also the works found in it are being exhibited. Also, the works found in the Seven Sleepers' Cavern are in this hall. In addition, the statue of the mother Goddess Cybele which belongs to 6th century B.C., and the stele of Olympia, the daughter of Diokles of 2nd century B.C. are other works that attract attention.

In the Artemis hall which is visited next, the statues of Artemis and the works found in the Temple of Artemis take place. Both statues of Artemis, one called the Great Artemis and the other called the Beautiful Artemis were found during

the excavations made at Ephesus Prytaneion. The Great Artemis is 2.92 m. tall and belongs to 2nd century A.D. and has a triple bonnet on her head. The Beautiful Artemis is 1.74 m. tall and is made about 50 years after the other and besides her, sacred animals take place. These statues, with their multibreasts, represent fertility. The golden goddess statue found in the excavations of the Temple of Artemis which is on display in the showcase belongs to 2nd century B.C. The ivory, baked soil, bronze and golden works belong to the period between 7th and 5th centuries B.C. and were left at the temple as vow articles. From here, it is proceeded to a hall where emperor cults and portraits are on display. The first statue seen in this hall is of 6th century A.D. and belongs to Consul Stephanos. Other portraits which belong to distinguished inhabitants of Ephesus belong to 3rd century A.D. 4 pieces of friezes which belong to Temple of Hadrianus of 3rd century are also being

garden is brought here from the Belevi Mausoleum which is at a distance of 11 km. from Selçuk. It is believed that this Mausoleum of 3rd century B.C., belongs to Antiochos Theos II, died in 246 B.C. in Ephesus, who is one of the kings of Seleukos after Alexander the Great. Today at the site of this Mausoleum which is 23 m. high and has dimensions

displayed in this hall. In the centre, a part of the altar of Domitian Temple can be seen. Also Julia Paula's bust, and the bust of emperors such as Commodus, Trajan, Nero, Germanicus and Augustus take place here. When we leave this hall after seeing the statues of Augustus and of his wife Livia we shall have completed our tour through the Museum.

Cave of the Seven Sleepers

A road leading past the Vedius Gymnasium directs eastwards towards the Cave of the Seven Sleepers. According to legend, seven young Christians living in the reign of the emperor Decius (around 250 A.D.) refused to offer the required sacrifices at the emperor's shrine, and escaped from the town to hide in this cave. Some time later they are said to have fallen asleep, and slept for so long that when they woke up and went out for food, they found that the city had completely changed, and along with it the emperor's rule. With some surprise they realise that they have been asleep for 200 years, and that Christianity has spread throughout Ephesus.

Two views of Seven Sleepers.

The new emperor, Theodosius, hearing of their tale, declared it a miracle that they had been raised from the dead, and their fame spread.

On their death, the seven sleepers are said to have been buried here in the same cave with funerary rites, and a church erected over the cave.

Excavations on the site revealed, in the walls and tombs of the 5-6th century church, a number of graves belonging to devotees to the seven sleepers, among them one thought to belong to St. Madeleine.

House of the Virgin Mary

Some four to six years after the death of Christ, St. John is said to have accompanied the Virgin Mary to Ephesus, where it is believed they dwelt in a small house over which now stands the Council Church, or the Church of the Virgin Mary. The Council Ephesus, dated of 431 record this. Later St. John brought the Virgin Mother to a house on the slopes of Bülbül Mountain, the position of which was later forgotten, until research was begun in 1891 to find traces of it. Katerina Emmerikin discovered this house at Panaya Kapulu, which fits the descriptions given in the sources. It was officially accepted to be the house of the Virgin in 1892 with the celebration of high mass there by Timoni, Archbishop of Izmir, and this belief has recently been confirmed by Pope Paul VI in 1967 and Pope John Paul II in 1979 with the celebration of high mass at Ephesus. The house is reached by a road leading from the ruins of Ephesus towards the Bülbül Mountain, and is only a short walk from the road (100 m).

On the site of the House of the Virgin Mary is a cruciform church with a central dome, which is thought to have been incorporated into the original building in the 6-7th centuries.

The later structure can easily be identified, as shown in red. Entering the church via an arched portico with flanking niches, one reaches a vaulted narthex, from which a raised portal leads to the nave and apse. A statue of the Virgin Mary to be seen here was erected in the last century, and is fronted by a grey hearth area, known to have been used for burning coal, and traces of coal and wine were found there during excavations. The small room to the south

Statue of the Virgin Mary.

was a bed chamber. The absidal niche in the eastern wall of this room is regarded as a shrine by Moslems, who believe in the saintliness of the Virgin Mary. Arabic inscriptions around the walls are quotations from the Koran relating to the Virgin Mary. To the west are a series of fountains springing from below the floor of the house. The water flowing from these fountains is considered curative. Visitors are free to drink the waters under the shade of the shrine.

Exterior and interior views of the Virgin Mary House.

Statue of the Virgin Mary.

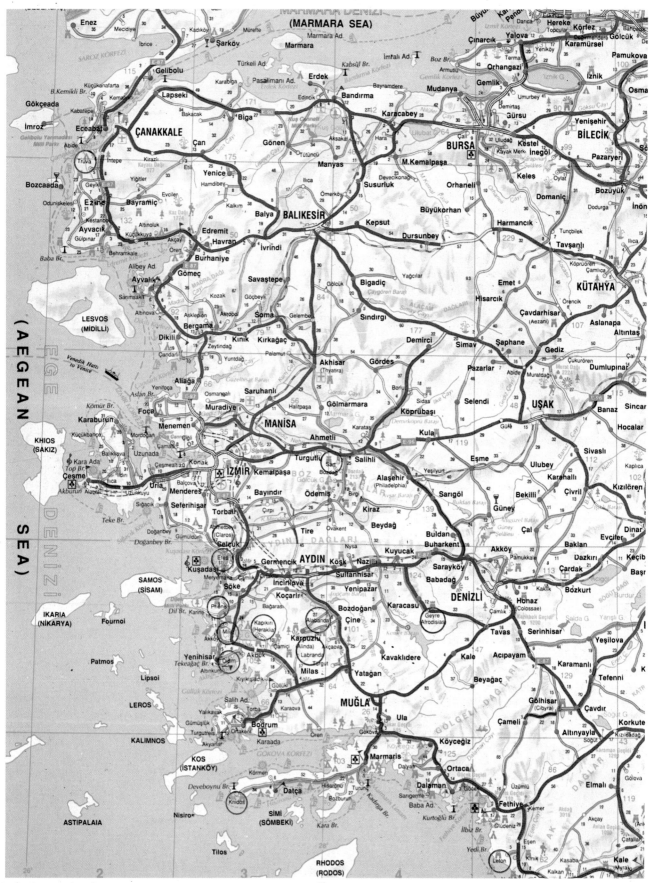

Map of western Anatolia.